Antlered Stag of Dawn

夜明けの牡鹿

Antlered Stag of Dawn

Haiku in Irish & English
by Gabriel Rosenstock

Translated into Scots by John McDonald
and into Japanese by Mariko Sumikura
with linocuts by Mathew Staunton

The Onslaught Press

Published in Oxford by The Onslaught Press
11 Ridley Road, OX4 2QJ
September, 2015

Texts © 2015 **Gabriel Rosenstock**, **John McDonald**,
and **Mariko Sumikura**

Cover and illustrations © 2015 **Mathew Staunton**

Many thanks to **J. Derrick McClure** and **Colm Ó Baoill**
of Aberdeen University for their invaluable help
with the Scottish Gaelic texts in this book

ISBN-13 **978-0-9927238-9-7**

Typeset in Hiragino Kaku Gothic Pro W3 & W6,
designed, & edited by **Mathew Staunton**

Printed by Lightning Source

The gendai haiku in this book came about after the writer was asked to become a Lineage Holder of Celtic Buddhism and on first beholding a photograph of the Very Venerable Chögyam Trungpa in Highland Regalia.

Notes to some of the haiku may be found at the end of the book.

Your kindly slope, with bilberries and blaeberries, studded with cloudberries that are round-headed and red; wild-garlic clusters in the corners of the rock terraces, and abounding tufted crags; the dandelion and pennyroyal, and the soft white bog-cotton and sweet-grass there on every part of it, from the lowest level to where the peaks are at the topmost edge. Fine is the clothing of Craig Mhór—there is no coarse grass for you there, but moss saxifrage of the juiciest covering it on this side and on that; the level hollows at the foot of the jutting rocks, where primroses and delicate daisies grow, are leafy, grassy, sweet and hairy, bristly, shaggy—every kind of growth there is. There is a shady fringe of green water-cresses around every spring that is in its lands, a sorrel thicket at the base of the rough rocks, and sandy gravel crushed small and white; gurgling and plunging, coldly boiling, in swirls of water from the foot of the smooth falls, the splendid streams with their blue-braided tresses come dashing and spirting in a swerving gush...

A. Macleod, *The Songs of Duncan Ban Macintyre* (Edinburgh, 1952), pp. 166-8.

Haiku

1

a chosantóir an domhain
ná hiompaigh d'aghaidh uainn—
francach óg sa chamras

protector of the world
do not turn your face from us—
young rat in the sewer

gairdian o the warl
dinnae turn awa fraes—
rattan i the jaw-hole

世界の保護者
我らから顔を背けるな—
下水の子鼠でも

nach dtiocfaidh tú go deo arís?
. . . níor imíos riamh
sioscadh sa ghiolcach

will ye no' come back again?
. . . I never left
whisper in the reeds

wull ye no cum back agane?
. . . a nivver quat
fusper i the sprots

戻りはすまい
葦むらに囁きなど
残しはすまい

an folús go léir
id' sparán folamh—
aiteann faoi bhláth

holder of all emptiness in your
empty sporran—
bloomin' heather

hauder o tuimness
i yer tuim sporran—
bleemin hedder

虚無の保持者よ
それは空財布―
花咲くヒース

taoisigh ar lár—
féach ort féin ag éirí—
carria mór an mhaidneachain

laid low are the chieftains
but see, you arise—
great stag of dawn

chieftens dung doon bit
leuk, resurrectit—
muckle stag o dawin

寝そべる族長
だが見よ　君は身を起こす
夜明けの牡鹿

the Gael's breathing space—on the summit!

anail a' Ghàidheil, air a mhullach!

the hielant chiel's scowthe—on the knowe-heid

ゲール（語）の息づく空間—山頂にあり！

led' sgian achlais
déan obráid intinne orainn go léir—
búir easa

with your mattucashlass
perform brain surgery on all—
waterfall roar

wi yer dirk
labotomize thaim aw—
linn rair

懐剣で
みなに脳味噌手術
瀧の轟きよ

is dearóil iad na caoráin
cá bhfuil na tinte cnámh?
gealach reoite

the moors are desolate
where are all the bonfires?
frozen moon

the muirs are gowstie
whaur're aw the banefires?
geelt muin

湿地荒れ
篝火いずこ
凍り月

led mhaothachán
bog an t-éadach do na mná—
faill ù hill ó hó ró éileadh

with your stale piss
soften cloth for the women—
faill ù hill ó hó ró éileadh

wi yer mingin pish
saften the claith fir the weemin—
faill ù hill ó hó ró éileadh

古尿（いばり）
女のために柔き衣
歌えや歌えファイル　ウ　ヒル　オ　ホ　ロ　イレ

mná na ngarbhchríoch
sciobfaidís an sgian dubh uait—
réalta an tráthnóna

highland women
they'd steal your black dagger—
evening star

heilant weemin
they'd pauchle yer bleck dirk—
eenin stern

高地 (ハイランド) の女ども
君の飾剣　盗みとる
宵の明星

fuisce—
duitse a deineadh é—
cearc fhraoigh sa chlapsholas

whiskey—
it was made for you—
grouse in the gloaming

ウイスキ─
君がためにぞ作らるる
黄昏の雷鳥よ

whuskie—
it wis wrocht fir ye—
groose i the gloamin

an domhan seo
an rud ait cruinn seo
babhla cantaireachta

this world
this queer round thing
singing bowl

this warl
this unco roond thingmy
dirlin bowlie

この世界
奇妙で丸いこのものは
歌う鉢

11

cúbann Ollphéist Loch Nis
go gasta uait—
ód' stánadh stuama

the Loch Ness Monster
retreats quickly—
your steady gaze

Nessie
taks leg—
yer steive glower

ネス湖の怪獣
すばやく逃げたり—
汝が凝視

少女のために君がいる
少女はニシンの腸（はらわた）取り―
君は腸代わりなり

tá tú ann dóibh
cailíní na scadán—
tá tú ann do na scadáin

you are there for them
girls gutting herrings—
you're there for the herrings

ye're thair fir thaim lassies
guttin herrin—
ye're thair fir the herrin

13

d'fhéach tusa, leis,
ar fheochadán, ar meisce,
fág an bealach!

drunk, you too
looked at a thistle
faugh a ballagh!

drucken, you tae
leukit at a thrissel
faugh a ballagh!

呑み過ぎだ　君も
アザミを見よ
フォ　ア　バラー

an triùir nach fuiling an cniadachadh
seann bhean, cearc, agus caora

three that won't bear caressing
an old woman, a hen, and a sheep

threy that winnae thole slaikin
a carline, a chookie, an a yowie

愛撫に耐えられぬこの三つ
老女　雌鳥　羊

réaltaí os cionn na hAlban
os cionn na Tibéide—
an saor dóibh?

stars over Scotland
over Tibet—
are they free?

sterns ower Scotia
ower Tibet—
hae they wan free?

スコットランドの空の星
チベットの空の星—
それらは自由

caoinigí
is gáirigí im' theannta—
eallach Gaelach

weep with me
laugh with me
shaggy highland cattle

greet wi me
lauch wi me
tousie hielant kye

共に泣け
共に笑え
毛羽立つハイランドの家畜たち

urraim is neamhurraim
téad rite a shiúlaímid le chéile—
hoips!

reverence and irreverence
the tight-rope we walk together—
oops!

敬意と不敬
我ら共々綱渡り—
おっと！

respeck an disrespeck
we traivel the tichtrowp thegither—
fegs!

do shaol gairid—
do shaol síoraí . . .
ceannbhán faoin ngealach lán

your short life—
your life eternal . . .
bog cotton under a full moon

yer jimpit life
yer life ayebydand . . .
bog cotton unner a fou muin

君　短命―
君　永遠の命・・・
満月下　沼の綿

leipreacháin!
an duine deireanach sa chruinne
a ghéill dóibh

leprechauns!
last man in the universe
to believe in them

the peerie fowk!
hinmaist chiel i the warl
tae believe i thaim

レプラコーン（小妖精）よ
宇宙で 最後の最後に
信じるにたる者よ

come with me, will you not come
to the woods of Hallaig?
time is a deer

tar liomsa tar, nach dtiocfá liom
go Hallaig, is an t-am
ann ina fhia!

cum wi me, wull ye no cum
tae the wuids o Hallaig?
time's a rae

付いてこい
ハライグの森へこないか？
時は鹿なり

foirm is ea folús
folús foirm—
tumann murúch

form is emptiness
emptiness form—
a mermaid dives

kythins are tuimness
tuimness kythins—
a marmaid dooks

形は無い
虚しい形—
人魚の飛込み

for auld lang's syne
cad is 'auld' ann?
stadann traonach dá chlamhsán

for auld lang's syne
what's 'auld'?
a corncrake ceases to complain

fir auld lang syne
whit's auld?
a craik quats channerin

オールド　ラング　ザインの
オールドは何？
ウズラクイナが不平を止む

chonaicís an teaspach
sa soipín féir, sa dreoilín—
labhair lena gcosantóirí

you saw the vigour
in a wisp of straw, in a wren
and spoke to their guardians

ye glisked the smeddum
in a tait o strae, in a wran,
an threipit tae thair gairdians

元気をみたぞ
一束の麦 ミソサザイに
守護神たちに話しかけた

áilleagán ar chrann Nollag
an domhan seo againne
i measc na ndomhan go léir

a bauble on a Christmas tree
this world of ours
among many

a geegaw on a Yule tree
this warl o oors
amang monie

クリスマスツリーの飾物
我らのためのこの世
あまたのなかに混じりおり

cad a thug go hÉirinn thú
go hAlbain? na huaisle?
'dubh leo!'

what brought you to Ireland,
to Scotland? fairies?
'thick with them!'

whit brung ye tae Ireland,
tae Scotia? hill fowk?
'thrang wi thaim!'

愛蘭国に　何をもたらす
スコットランドに？妖精か？
「それらを満たせ！」

níl aon ní a tháinig ó do bhéal
nár choinnigh an caonach slán—
léicean

nothing from your mouth
that is not preserved by moss—
lichen

naethin frae yer mou
that isnae hained bi fog—
crottle

君の無音
苔に遮られたわけじゃあるまい—
地衣よ

admhaigh é—
is fearr seacht n-uaire é fuisce
ná bainne geaca . . . fós féin . . .

admit it—
whiskey is seven times better
than yak's milk . . . and yet . . .

awn up—
whuskie's seiven times better
nor yak's mulk . . . an yit . . .

認めるよ―
ウイスキーはヤク乳より七倍良し
だがなあ・・・

cad a chualaís sa phíb mhór
grá? sléacht? bua? cliseadh?
há há

what was it you heard in the bagpipes?
love? war? triumph? defeat?
ha ha

whit wis't ye hearkent tae i the pipes?
luve? weir? veectory? defait?
ha ha

バグパイプに何を聞いた？
愛か 戦か 勝利 敗北？
ハハハ

"mo thrua ort, a thír,
tá an chaora mhór ag teacht!"
an tusa a labhair?

"woe to thee, my country,
the great sheep are coming!"
was it you who spoke?

"wae tae ma kintra,
the muckle yowes're comin!"
wis't ye that spak?

「汝に災難　わが祖国に
偉大な羊　来たりたり！」
語りしは汝なりしか？

sea-eagle!
what fish is in its talons?
holy mouth agape

fiolar mara!
cén t-iasc é sin ina chrobh?
béal beannaithe ar leathadh

ウミワシよ！
鉤爪の魚は何だった？
聖なる口がパックリ開く

earn!
whit fush is in'ts cleuks?
haly mou apen

'caisteal ciar Chulchallaigh
fuar, falamh . . .'
ag feitheamh led' bhriathar

'the stern castle of Kilcoy
cold and empty . . .'
awaiting your word

'the dour castle o Kilcoy
cauld an tuim . . .'
bidein a wurd

「いかめしきキルコイ城
冷たく空虚・・・」
君の言葉を待っている

thair wullnae be yin wice chiel
amang a thoosand gowks

there will not be one wise man
among a thousand fools

cha bhi aon duine crìonna
am measg mìle amadan

一人の賢人も出ないだろう
この何千もの愚者のなかからは

31

Drala! d'each bán
siúd thall é! fionncheo!
ag éirí is ag titim . . .

Drala! your white steed
he's there! he's mist!
rising, falling . . .

Drala! yer fite cuddy
he's thair! he's haar!
heavin up, fawin . . .

ドララ！君の白馬は
そこにいる　霧だ
上昇し　下降す

an rabhais ann
nuair a cailleadh Uallas?
cuirliún ag glaoch ón ngleann

were you there
when Wallace died?
a curlew calls from the glen

そこに君はありしか
ウォーレスの死に際に
シギが谷から呼んでいる

wur ye thair
whan Wallace dee'd?
a whaup cries frae the glen

léim bláthanna
as ithir gheimhridh
is rugadh thú i stábla

flowers sprang up
from winter soil
and you were born in a stable

flooers kythed
frae wunter sile
an ye wur born in a byre

花芽を吹く
冬土から
君が生れし畜舎のなかで

ciorcal liag—
iad siúd a rinc duit tráth
fós ag rince

stone circle—
those who danced here once
still dance for you

stane-circle—
whae daunced here yince
aye daunce fir ye

ストーンサークル
かつて舞いたる者達が
今なお踊る君のため

cé a leanfadh thú?
níl éinne éinne—
patraisc sa sneachta

who can follow you?
nobody nobody—
partridge in the snow

whae can follae ye?
naebody naebody—
paitrick i the snaw

君を追うていくのは誰か
誰も　誰もいない
雪の山鶉

fia mór na mbeann
ag stánadh ar fhíor na spéire—
an tríú súil

the antlered stag
looks far into the horizon—
third eye

the antlered stag
goves faur intae the easin—
thurd ee

角つけた牡鹿が
遥か遠くの地平を見てる―
第三の目

an fhírinne, led' thoil!
píb mhór á seinm ag babhdán
. . . meán oíche

truth! please, the truth!
a scarecrow playing the pipes
. . . midnight

truith! please the truith!
a tattie-bogle doodlin the pipes
. . . midnicht

真実！ どうか、 真実を！
案山子がパイプを吹いている
・・・真夜中に

faoileáin ag éamh ó thuaidh i Steòrnabhagh
an t-éamh céanna
amach anseo

seagulls cry in far Stornoway
next year and the year after
the same cry

maws skirl in faur Stornoway
neist year an the year efter
the samen skirl

遠くのストロノウエイでカモメが啼く
来年も再来年も
同じ啼き声

samsara—birth and death
do we have the foggiest notion?
pale sun sinks

samsara—breith is bás
an bhfuil aon tuairim againn?
grian bhán ag dul faoi

輪廻―生と死
我らに迷霧の観ありや？
薄い陽が沈む

samsara—birth an daith
hae we onie notion?
paewae sin slumps

主よ遠吠え犬から月を護り給え

may the Almichtie hain the muin frae the dugs

gun gleidheadh an Tighearna a' ghealach bho na coin

may the Lord preserve the moon from the dogs

the Northern Lights   tartan of the clan

na Saighneáin   breacán na clainne

merry dancers   tartan o the clan

オーロラが氏族のタータンチェックを照らしている

bán: tuartha bán
bratach Mheiriceá
ar an ngealaigh

white: bleached white
the American flag
on the moon

fite: bleachit fite
the American flag
on the muin

白い色：褪せた白
米国旗
月のうえ

glóir na maidine   grian inti   ó am
annalód

in the morning glory   the sun   from ages
past

in the mornin glory　　the sin
　　　frae langsyne

朝顔のなか　　太陽は　　幾時代を
　　　過ぎゆきぬ

na saighneáin (arís)
teachtaireacht ó na déithe?
cá bhfios dáiríre?

the northern lights (again)
a message from the gods?
who really knows?

merry dancers (agane)
news frae the goads?
whae kens?

オーロラは（再び言おう）
神からの伝言か？
誰が真のそれを知る？

wunds dee awa
the seg is lown
the stag waukent

風絶えぬ
菅静まりて微動だにせず
牡鹿目覚める

gaotha ag éag
an chíb gan chorraí
an carria ina dhúiseacht

winds die away
sedge perfectly still
the stag awake

ardaigh an claíomh mór
chun na spéartha—
bagair ar na déithe!

hyst the claymore
tae the heivens—
threiten the goads!

lift the claymore
to the heavens—
threaten the gods!

天まで届けと
剣つき上げる―
神を脅さん

The Winter is Past
amhrán a thaitin leat . . .
conas tá ag Rabbie Burns?

The Winter is Past
a favourite song . . .
how fares Rabbie Burns?

The Winter Is Past
a weill-faured sang . . .
hou fares Rabbie Burns?

冬去りぬ
馴染みの歌よ・・・
ロビー・バーンズ今いかに？

SCANNAL GNÉIS!
dhá fheithid le chéile
ar pheiteal róis a thit

SEX SCANDAL!
two insects together
on a fallen rose petal

HOUGHMAGANDIE CLATTER!
twa beasties thegither
on a faw'n rose petal

セックススキャンダル！
二匹の虫が
薔薇の花びら落ちた上に

冬のスコットランド
少なくとも
君の息が見られる

Albain sa gheimhreadh
ar a laghad ar bith tá seans
d'anáil 'fheiscint

Scotia in wunter
yer lik
tae glisk yer braith

Scotland in winter
at least there's a chance
to see your breath

tha taobh dubh is taobh geal air
mar a bh'air bàta Mhic Iain Gheàrr*

  he has a white side and a black side
  like Mac Iain Ghearr's boat

he hus a fite side an a bleck side
like Mac Iain Ghearr's boatie

  彼はマックアイアン・ゲールの船のように
  白い側と黒い側をもっている

* Mac Iain Gheàrr, whose name means 'the son of Short John', also known as Archibald MacDonald, was a sea rover on the west coast of Scotland. When seen to leave on one of his raids, a watch was set, ready to capture him on his return. But the white boat that departed was black on her return and he got away with his exploits in this manner

tine ghealáin!
seo linn á hiniúchadh
is gearr ár ré

will-o'-the-wisp!
come, let us investigate
our time is short

daith cannle!
cum, let us speir oot
oor time's scant

なんたることぞ！
さあ来い　我ら検問せん
時は短し

éan a stánann ar an ré
i gcaitheamh na hoíche
an dtugtar freagraí di?

bird that stares at the moon
all night—what answers
is she given?

burd that glowers at the muin
aw nicht—whit repone
is she gien?

月をみつめる鳥
夜っぴて―どんな答えが
得らるるか？

labhair linn faoin Aigéan Mór!
lachain ag luipearnach
chun na linne

speak to us
of the Great Ocean: ducks waddling
to a pond

threip tae's
o the Muckle Tide: deuks hoddlin
tae a dub

語れかし
大洋のこと：アヒルよちよち
池に行く

dhá bhadhbh
ina suí ar ghéag
is an teagasc faoi chaibidil acu

twa corbies
sitting on a branch
discussing the teachings

烏二羽
枝に止まりて
教えを論ず

twa corbies
hunkert on a brainch
communin ower the teachins

53

下りろ下りろ
冷たい深海で　慰めを
パトリック・スペンス卿よ

doun gae doun
an ease'm i the cauld deep—
Sir Patrick Spens

down go down
and comfort him in the cold deep—
Sir Patrick Spens

síos leat síos
tabhair sólás dó sa duibheagán fuar—
Sir Patrick Spens

damhán alla i bpluais
an bua láimh linn
saor fá dheoidh

spider in a cave
victory at hand
free at last

attercap in a cave
veectory at haun
lowse at lang an last

洞窟のクモ
手にした勝利
ついには自由

imphléascadh an ama
faoina mheáchan féin—
Coinneach Odhar

when time collapses
under its own weight—
the Brahan Seer

whan time foonders
unner its ain wecht—
the Brahan Seer

時が廃れる
自らの重みのために—
ブラハン・セールの言*

aer úr na maidine
an tost briste—
clonscairt na mbeann

crisp morning
silence broken—
clash of antlers

keen mornin
lown tasht—
slash o antlers

パリパリした朝
破られた静けさ—
角突き合う音

om mane padme hūm
beacha stuama i measc
bhlátha samhraidh

om mane padme hūm
sober bees among
summer flowers

om mane padme hūm
sober bummers amang
simmer flooers

オム・マニ・ペメ・フム*
き真面目な蜂たち
夏花のなか

*チベット仏教の真言

pléascann Mars
amach as scamall dubh—
manach eile féindóite

Mars bursts out
from a dark cloud—
another monk self-immolated

Mars spleuters oot
frae a derk clud—
anither monk sel-secrifeest

火星爆発す
黒い雲から―
もう一人いたぞ ふしだら僧が

spideog ar maidin:
'Padmasambhava—
rugadh i loiteog é!'

a robin's morning song:
'Padmasambhava—
born in a lotus!'

Reid Rab's mornin sang:
'Padmasambhava—
born in a lotus!'

駒鳥 朝一番の歌
「パドマサンバヴァ—
蓮にご生誕！」

*チベット仏教「蓮華生大師」

stray dog! i know you
you listen to the birdies
to your own barking!

a mhadra strae! aithním thú
éisteann tú leis na héin
led' thafann féin

迷い犬よ　我知りたり
遠吠えに鳥が啼き応ず
汝がそを聴くを

stray dug! a ken ye
ye hearken tae burdies
tae yer ain bowfin

I am too accustomed to a wood   to be afraid of an owl

tha mi nas eòlaiche air coille   na bhith fo eagal na caillich-oidhche

余りに森に慣れすぎた　フクロウに怯えることに慣れすぎた

ower aquaint wi a wuid

tae be feart o a hoolet

canann lon trína ghob buí
scol na beatha, scol an bháis
nóta amháin

through its yellow beak
a blackbird sings a song of life
of death: one note

throuch its yalla neb
a bleckie croons a sang o life
o daith: yin spatril

黄い嘴から
黒歌鳥生を歌う 死を歌う
一本調子で

d'éirigh an ghrian
os cionn na Gainséise
a bhuíochas do Scarlatti

the sun rose
over the Ganges—
thanks entirely to Scarlatti

the sin raise
ower the Ganges—
thanks haillie tae Scarlatti

日は昇りぬ
ガンジス川に―
スカルラッティに深謝！

cosain an céadchosach
is míorúilt é—
        cosain míorúiltí

protect the centipede
it is a miracle—
        protect miracles

proteck Meg Monifeet
it's a meeracle—
        proteck meeracles

ムカデを守れ
それは奇跡だ──
　　　　　奇跡は守れ

tá mo chroí i nGarbhchríocha
na hAlban, na Tibéide
gaotha fuara ag séideadh

my heart's in the Highlands
of Scotland, Tibet—
cold winds blow

ma hert's i the hielants
o Scotia, Tibet—
snell wunds blaw

我が心は高地にあり
スコットランドやチベットの—
冷たい風吹く

gaotha
gaotha ársa ag éirí
an ruaigfear an leath ré?

winds
ancient winds rising
will they chase away the half moon?

wunds
auncient wunds tak up
wull they chase awa the hauf muin?

風よ
古代の風が立ち揚る
半月を吹き払うだろうか？

66

lá lá lá lá lá
lá lá lá lá lá lá lá
lá lá lá láma

la la la la la
la la la la la la la
la la la lama

ラララララ
ラララララララ
ララララマ

páistí, nuachair
bóiní Dé—
cá n-imíonn siad go léir?

children, spouses
ladybirds—
where do they all go?

bairns, marraes,
ladylanders—
whaur dae they aw gae?

子供よ　連れ合いよ
テントウムシよ―
お前たち　皆どこへ行く

cosain an t-aingeal
cosain an deamhan
an briathar! cosain é

protect the angel
protect the demon
the word! protect it

proteck the angel
proteck the wirricow
the wurd! proteck an aw

天使を守れ
悪魔を守れ
言葉よ！これを守れ

"tha biadh is ceòl an so, " mar a thuirt am madadh ruadh
's e ruith air falbh leis a' phìob

as the fox said, when running away with the bagpipes
there's meat and music here

狐の言うとおりだ、ここに肉と音楽がある
バグパイプが鳴れば遁走

there's mait an maisic here
as tod threipit rinnin frae the pipes

ithimis go léir
cloigeann caorach—
má má má má

let's all eat
a sheep's head—
ma ma ma ma

lat's aw lay till
a yowie's heid—
ma ma ma ma

たらふく食おう
羊の脳みそ—
ウメェ　メェ　メェ　メェ

71

彼が来る　彼が来る
ルンタの旗─何をもって来る？
風馬だ

seo chugainn, seo chugainn é
an *lungta*—cad tá aige?
each gaoithe

he comes, he comes
the *lungta*—what does he bring?
wind horse

he cums, he cums
the *lungta*—whit hus he brocht?
wund cuddie

leaves and branches
of the juniper—we'll burn them
on your return

duilleoga is géaga
an aitil—dóimis iad
ar theacht ar ais duit

leaves an brainches
o the jenepere—we'll brenn thaim
on yer retour

ネズの木の葉や枝も
焼き尽くそう
君が戻るとき

.

let not the white yak
become wild
and make smithereens of the mountains

na lig don gheac bán
éirí fiáin
is na sléibhte go léir a bhascadh

lat no the fite yak
turn willyart
an mak shivereens o the bens

白ヤクを
野生に目覚めさせるな
山々の粉塵とするな

brúchtann
inchinn an tsléibhe—
sneachta, criostail dhraíochta sneachta

the brains
of the mountain erupt—
snow, magic crystals of snow

the harns
o the ben erupt—
snaw, gramarie kirstals o snaw

山の噴火の
脳髄の―
雪だ　魔的な雪の結晶

naonúr iníonacha
bhandia na gcloch sneachta—
ag marcaíocht ar chuacha!

nine daughters
of the hail goddess—
all of them riding cuckoos!

nine dochters
o the hailstane goddess—
aw ridin gowks

雹（ひょう）の女神の
九人の娘—
みなカッコウに乗ってくる

manach ar leaba a bháis
ag feitheamh le scréach
iolar eitilte

monk on his death bed
awaiting the screech
of a flying squirrel

monk at the hinnerend
bidein the skreek
o a fleein-skwurrel

死の床の僧
飛びさるリスの
キーキー声を待ちたり

ritheann, stopann,
ritheann an tslí eile—
luch ag lorg saoirse

running, stopping,
running the other way—
mouse in search of freedom

rinnin, stappin,
rinnin widdershins—
moose reengin fir scowth

走る　止まる
また別方向に走る─
自由を探す小鼠よ

cosain an cuileann
na caora beannaithe—
páiste laomleicneach

protect the holly
the sacred berries—
flame-cheeked child

proteck the hollin
the sacred berries—
lowe-chaftit bairn

モチの木を守れ
神聖な実を守れ―
赤いほっぺの子供を守れ

cén sólás
do Meg Merrilees é? gan suipéar
stánann ar an ngealach

what comfort
for Meg Merrilees? supperless
she stares at the moon

whit easement
fir Meg Merrilees? sipperless
she goves at the muin

何の慰めがある
メグ・メリーズに 食もせず
ただ月影を見つめてる

oíche dhorcha—faic
gan spéartha aislingeacha
Sonojo fiú

black night—nothing at all
not even the dream-skies
of Sonojo

bleck nicht—naethin at aw
no even the drame-lifts
o Sonojo

暗夜だ—なにも見えない
夢の夜空すらない
あのソノージョの

an chéad bhraon báistí
a thit riamh
inár gcroí go dtite sé

the first raindrop
ever to fall
may it fall in our heart

the furst spark
  ivver tae faw
    may it faw in oor hert

最初の雨粒
  いつものとおり
    心の中に落ちますように

the first note ever
from a bagpipe—
the teachings

an chéad nóta riamh
ón bpíb mhór—
an teagasc

最初の調べは
常にバグパイプから——
数々の教訓

the furst spatril ivver
frae the pipes—
the teachins

83

湯気たつ糞山―
雄鶏が調教している
複雑な演戯を

steaming dunghill—
a cock is practising
dressage

reekin midden—
a rooster practeeses
dressage

gal ón gcarn aoiligh—
dreasáiste á chleachtadh
ag coileach

liotharach
de dhuilleoga lofa á reo
cioróis ae

a mush of rotten leaves
begins to freeze
cirrhosis of the liver

a powsowdie o mozie leaves
sterts tae geel
cirrhosis o the liver

粥状の腐れ葉が
凍り始める
肝硬変

á nguthú féinig
á saolú féinig
na chéad phréacháin

voicing themselves
giving birth to themselves
the first crows

vycin thirsels
gien birth tae thirsels
the furst craws

独言の声
己が誕生
カラスの初啼き

chan eil am bàs na iongantas
no Ifrinn mar a dh'aithrisear*

death is nothing wonderful
nor is Hell as it is said to be

daith is naethin wunnerfae
nor is hell as we'd jalouse

死より不思議なものはない
地獄では言われていやしないが

* When Colm Cille founded his monastery in Iona, it was revealed to him that he would have to bury one of his fellow-monks alive as a sacrifice, if the mission were to succeed. St Oran promptly volunteered, as would any decent Irishman in the circumstances. After three days and three nights, Colm Cille ordered the grave to be opened. St Oran looked up and uttered the words above. Colm Cille couldn't believe his ears. "Tuilleadh ùr air Ordhain!" said he. "Pile more earth on Oran!"

as though
resting: an abandoned
fishing boat

faoi mar a bheadh
scíth á ligean aici
bád iascaigh tréigthe

あたかも
休むがごとく：乗り棄てられた
漁船

as though
restin: forleitit
drave boat

87

Eige
cad tá á rá
ag Traigh a' Bhìgeil?

isle of Eigg
what say they?
singing sands

isle o Eigg
whit dae they threip?
croonin saunds

エッグ島
何を語るや
鳴き砂は

fearthainn os
Loch Fìne
ag sileadh de smut dobharchú

rain over
Lough Fyne
streaming from an otter's snout

weet ower
Loch Fyne
teemin frae an otter's snoot

雨止みぬ
ファインの湖水
カワウソの鼻から湯気

a bird! the students say. not at all!
the sky and a bird flying through it

éan! a deir na daltaí. ní hea mhuise!
spéir is éan ag eitilt tríthi

V

a burd! the collegianer crys. naw naw!
the lift an a burd fleein throuch it

鳥だ！　学生たち言う　そうじゃない！
空と　突っ切っていく鳥さ

oilte ar haiku
ní bheireann an garda ort—
PLAB! ar do cheann

a haiku-trained bodyguard
fails to catch you!
PLOP! you fall on your head

a haiku-lairnt luchtach
misses ye!
PLOP! ye faw on yer heid

俳句修行のガードマン
君をつかまえそこねて
ポチャン！君は頭から落ちたのさ

néal muisiriúnach—
gob an phréacháin
ar leathadh

mushroom cloud—
the crow's mouth
agape

puddock stuil clud—
the craw's mou
apen

原爆雲—
カラスの口が
パクっとあく

dhá phónaí bhreaca
i gcoill—
grian íseal na Samhna

two piebald ponies
in a wood . . .
low November sun

twa pyot pownies
in a wuid . . .
laich November sin

二頭の若い斑馬
森の中に
霜月の太陽 低し

among dandelions
the blackbird's beak
vanishes

i measc na gcaisearbhán
gob an loin
ag dul as amharc

amang pish-the-beds
the bleckie's neb
vainishes

タンポポのなかへ
カラスの嘴が
消える

shadow of the bumble bee
on a morning glory—
where are our ancestors?

scáil na bumbóige
ar ghlóir na maidine—
cá bhfuil ár sinsir?

ブンブン蜂の影が
朝顔の上に―
我らの祖先は今何処？

sheddae o the bummer
on a mornin glory—
whaur're oor forebeirs?

cosain an uile ní beo!
éan i ndris, éan,
éan i ndris

protect all living things!
bryd one brere, brid,
brid one brere

proteck aw leevin things!
bryd one brere, brid,
brid one brere

生きとし生けるものを守れ
野バラの上の小鳥よ　小鳥
野バラに憩う小鳥よ

96

Gleann Fhionghain
is corrrach iad na scamaill
san uisce

Glenfinnan
clouds are restless
in the water

Glenfinnan
cluds're fykie
in the watter

グレンフィナン渓谷
雲は休まず
水の上

cúig lá i ndiaidh do bháis
teas fós id chroí—
eitlíonn cuach ó thuaidh

five days after your death
your heart still warm—
a cuckoo flies north

five days efter yer daith
yer hert aye tosie—
a gowk flees north

君逝きて五日
心臓はまだ温かい―
カッコーが北へ飛ぶ

loime na gcrann
ag tnúth le duilliúr—
Gúrú

bareness of trees
yearning for foliage—
Guru

scabbit treen
greenin fir fulyerie—
Guru

木の洞は
葉枝憧れ—
グル （導師）よ

duilliúr
ag tnúth le loime—
Gúrú Gúrú

yearning of foliage
for bareness—
Guru Guru

greenin o fulyerie
fir scabbitness—
GURU GURU

枝葉の憧れは
裸木なり―
グルよ　グルよ

duilliúr ag tnúth le duilliúr
loime le loime—
Gúrú Gúrú Gúrú

foliage yearning for foliage
bareness for bareness—
Guru Guru Guru

fulyerie greenin fir fulyerie
scabbitness fir scabbitness
Guru Guru Guru

枝葉は枝葉を憧れる
裸木は裸木を憧れる
グルよ　グルよ　グルよ

Notes

2 'Will ye no' come back again', also known as 'Bonnie Charlie', is a Scots song. Everyone should listen to it (or sing it) at least once in a lifetime. Try the Ewan MacColl and Peggy Seeger recording.

3 *Sporran* is Scottish Gaelic for 'purse' and is worn on the kilt, acting as a pocket.

5 A *mattucashlass* is a dagger held in the sleeve.

7 In a waulking song, women worked together on new tweed, beating it to soften it: *faill ù hill ó hó ró éileadh* is a typical refrain or vocable.

8 The *sgian dubh*, a small, black knife, is part of traditional Highland dress.

11 'The Very Venerable Chögyam Trungpa was an admirer of the Irish saint-druid, Colm Cille (Columba) whose encounter with the Loch Ness Monster in the year 565 is recorded by his hagiographer:

> On another occasion also, when the blessed man was living for some days in the province of the Picts, he was obliged to cross the river Nesa; and when he reached the bank of the river, he saw some of the inhabitants burying an unfortunate man, who, according to the account of those who were burying him, was a short time before seized, as he was swimming, and bitten most severely by a monster that lived in the water; his wretched body was, though too late, taken out with a hook, by those who came to his assistance in a boat.
>
> The blessed man, on hearing this, was so far from being dismayed, that he directed one of his companions to swim over and row across the coble that was moored at the farther bank.

And Lugne Mocumin hearing the command of the excellent man, obeyed without the least delay, taking off all his clothes, except his tunic, and leaping into the water.

But the monster, which, so far from being satiated, was only roused for more prey, was lying at the bottom of the stream, and when it felt the water disturbed above by the man swimming, suddenly rushed out, and, giving an awful roar, darted after him, with its mouth wide open, as the man swam in the middle of the stream.

Then the blessed man observing this, raised his holy hand, while all the rest, brethren as well as strangers, were stupefied with terror, and, invoking the name of God, formed the saving sign of the cross in the air, and commanded the ferocious monster, saying, 'Thou shalt go no further, nor touch the man; go back with all speed.' Then at the voice of the saint, the monster was terrified, and fled more quickly than if it had been pulled back with ropes, though it had just got so near to Lugne, as he swam, that there was not more than the length of a spear-staff between the man and the beast.

Then the brethren seeing that the monster had gone back, and that their comrade Lugne returned to them in the boat safe and sound, were struck with admiration, and gave glory to God in the blessed man ...

12 An allusion to a famous poem by Gaelic poet Derick Thompson (Ruaraidh MacThòmais).

13 An allusion to a famous poem by Scots poet Hugh Mac Diarmid. The last line, *faugh a ballagh*, is an anglicised form of an Irish-Scottish battle-cry which translates as, 'Clear the way!' It was made famous by one Sergeant Patrick Masterson who made the cry before seizing the French Imperial Eagle during the Battle of Barossa, thereafter proclaiming, "Be Japers, boys! I have the Cuckoo!"

19 An allusion to a famous poem by Gaelic poet Sorley MacLean (Somhairle Mac Gill-Eathain).

21 An allusion to a famous song by Robert Burns.

28 Prophecy, or Second Sight, was not unusual in the Highlands of Scotland.

29 The sea-eagle is sacred as it catches the salmon: *eo* is the old Irish word for salmon, the root of *eolas*, 'knowledge'.

30 The words of the Brahan Seer (the Nostradamus of Scotland).

31 Drala, Chögyam Trungpa Rinpoche's white horse. For a definition of drala, please see: http://www.glossary.shambhala.org/#DRALA

32 Uilliam Uallas or William Wallace was a 13th-century Scottish freedom fighter and subject of the film *Braveheart*.

50 A reference to the chakor.

52 An allusion to a medieval Scots ballad.

53 An allusion to a fine old Scottish ballad. Gabriel Rosenstock's Irish translation of this song: http://recmusic.org/lieder/get_texts.html?Contribl d=1031

54 An allusion to the legend of Bruce and the spider.

55 An allusion to Coinneach Odhar or the Brahan Seer. See 30 above.

58 Please see: http://www.savetibet.org/resources/fact-sheets/self-immolations-by-tibetans/

59 A reference to an 8th-century patriarch of Tibetan Buddhism.

60 An allusion to a beautiful poem by Chögyam Trungpa in which he addresses himself as a stray dog, a befriender of birds and jackals. Here is an Irish transcreation of the same poem:

Madra Strae

Chögyam, níl ann ach madra strae
Ar fán timpeall na cruinne,
San aigéan, mám sneachta i measc na mbeann.
Ar aghaidh leis ina mhadra strae
Gan aon chuimhneamh aige ar an gcéad bhéile eile.
Beidh sé mór leis na héin is leis na seacáil
Is le hainmhí fiáin ar bith.

62 An allusion to a song by Scarlatti. Here is the anonymous Italian text followed by Gabriel Rosenstock's version in Irish:

Già il sole dal Gange
Più chiaro sfavilla,
E terge ogni stilla
Dell'alba che piange.

Col raggio dorato
Ingemma ogni stello,
E gli astri del cielo
Dipinge nel prato.

Os cionn abhainn na Gainséis'
an ghrian gheal ag lonrú,
Is glanann gach deoir úr
den láchan tá 'caoineadh.

Le gaetha fíor-órga
an féar glas á mhaisiú;
Sa spéir gheal na réaltaí
á bpéinteáil sa mhóinéar.

64 An allusion to a famous poem by Robert Burns.

My heart's in the Highlands, my heart is not here,
My heart's in the Highlands a-chasing the deer—
chasing the wild deer, and following the roe;
My heart's in the Highlands, wherever I go.

Farewell to the Highlands, farewell to the North
The birth place of Valour, the country of Worth;
Wherever I wander, wherever I rove,
The hills of the Highlands for ever I love.

Farewell to the mountains high cover'd with snow;
Farewell to the straths and green valleys below;
Farewell to the forests and wild-hanging woods;
Farwell to the torrents and loud-pouring floods.

66 This haiku was ceremoniously buried in a place called Samya. The times we live in are not yet ripe for it.

67 The word 'la' in Tibetan denotes 'life spirit'.

68 The Irish for a ladybird is 'bóín Dé', 'God's little cow'. The same concept exists in Welsh and Russian.

70 'Yang' is the Tibetan word for 'prosperity spirit' and also the word for a sheep. The third line of this haiku was inspired by the incomparable singing of the Tenore di Oniferi: http://www.ckuik.com/tenore_di_oniferi

71 Exoterically speaking, the wind horse refers to the pony express. A postal system. For an esoteric explanation of the wind horse in the teachings of the Dorje Dradul of Mukpo (Chögyam Trungpa Rinpoche) please consult: http://www.glossary.shambhala.org/#WINDHORSE

73 It is not clear what Rosenstock has in mind with this haiku (if, indeed, his mind was functioning at all*). He may be referring to yar-lha-sham-po, a fierce mountain god who resisted the first Buddhist missionaries, fog emanating from his nostrils and so on. *The following haiku, No. 74, suggests that something may have gone wrong with Rosenstock's brain and No. 75 only confirms our suspicions.

75 What would Sergeant Masterson (no. 13) make of it all?

76 An allusion to Hōjō, who on hearing the flying squirrel, is said to have addressed his brethren thus: 'This is what it's all about, folks! This penetrating immediacy. This is exactly what must be understood and remembered. Nothing else. Now I can depart.' And he did.

79 An allusion to the following stanza in a poem by Keats:

> No breakfast had she many a morn,
>   No dinner had she many a noon
> And 'stead of supper she would stare
>   Full hard against the moon.

80 An allusion to a disciple of Bashō. She was an eye doctor and in her death-verse she wonders if the skies of a lifetime were real or not.

87 Walk on it when it is dry and the quartz beach squeaks!

95 An allusion to one of the earliest English love lyrics. The words *bryd one brere, brid, brid one brere* translate as 'bird on briar, bird, bird on briar'. It may well be, however, that a Celtic Goddess of Light, Brigitta—later the illustrious Irish saint, Bríd—is also concealed in the invocation. Here are the three stanzas of the ancient song and Gabriel's Irish translation:

Bird on a Briar

> Bryd one brere, brid, brid one brere,
> Kynd is come of love, love to crave
> Blythful biryd, on me thu rewe
> Or greyth, lef, greith thu me my grave.

Hic am so blithe,
so bryhit, brid on brere,
Quan I se that hende in halle:
Yhe is whit of lime, loveli, trewe
Yhe is fayr and flur of alle.

Mikte ic hire at wille haven,
Stedefast of love, loveli, trewe,
Of mi sorwe yhe may me saven
Ioye and blisse were were me newe.

Éan i nDriseog

Éan, éan i ndriseog, éan, éan i ndriseog,
Den ghrá é an cine, an grá sea a thnúth,
Éinín suairc, orm glac trua
Nó réitigh dom, a ghrá, an uaigh.

Is suairc a bhímse, is geal, éan i ndriseog,
Nuair a chímse an bhé úd sa halla,
Is bán é a cneas, aoibhinn, síodúil,
Sí an plúr í, is sí is áille.

Dá mbeadh sí agam an bhé dom féinig
Daingean i ngrá, aoibhinn, síodúil,
Fáth mo bhuartha, is í an réiteach
Suairc is séimh a bheinnse go síoraí.

96 Glenfinnan: The village which witnessed the
beginning of the Jacobite Rising (1745)

The Participants

Gabriel Rosenstock was born in 1949 in postcolonial Ireland. Poet, playwright, haikuist, essayist, and author/translator of over 180 books, mostly in Irish, he is a member of Aosdána, a Lineage Holder of Celtic Buddhism, and an Honorary Member of the European Haiku Society. He has taught haiku at the Schule für Dichtung, Vienna, and Hyderabad Literary Festival. He blogs at http://roghaghabriel.blogspot.ie

Mariko Sumikura is a poet and essayist born in Kyoto in 1952. She graduated from Ristumeikan University and is a representative of the Japan Universal Poets Association and editor of online international journal *Poetic-Bridge: Ama-Hashi* and Junpa Books. Her publications include *Kokoro Kaoru Hito*, *Yume Tsumugu Hito*, *Hikari Oru Hito*, *Ai Matou Hito*, and *Tsuchi daku Masurao*. She participated in the 49th Struga Poetry Readings (Macedonia, 2011), Jan Smrek International Literary Festival (Slovakia, 2012), and Europa in Verci (Como, Italy, 2015). In 2012 she was awarded a translation stipend by the Ireland Literature Exchange for *Mina wo Tonaete* (*Uttering Her Name* by Gabriel Rosenstock).

John McDonald came to haiku in the mid-nineties, fell in love with the genre, and never left: it fitted so well with the musicality of the Scots language (and perhaps the love of some Scots of speaking as few words as possible). He has a bi-lingual blog which he tries to update daily: http://zenspeug.blogspot.com

Mathew Staunton is a printmaker and editor originally from Coolock in Dublin. Now based in Oxford, he makes books and prints in his workshop at the bottom of the garden.

Lightning Source UK Ltd.
Milton Keynes UK
UKOW04f0113030316

269466UK00001B/14/P